My
Listening
Ears

Library of Congress Cataloging in Publication Data

De Jonge, Joanne E., 1943–
    My listening ears.

    (My father's world)
    Summary: A collection of twenty-four short essays describing
unique facts about the intestines, pituitary gland, nerves, and
other parts of the human body and discussing how they reflect
the wonder of God.

    1. Body, Human—Religious aspects—Christianity—
Addresses, essays, lectures—Juvenile literature. 2. Creation—
Addresses, essays, lectures—Juvenile literature. [1. Body,
Human—Religious aspects—Christianity] I. Bishop, Richard, ill.
II. Title. III. Series.
BT743.D4   1985   233'.5   85-7372
ISBN 0-930265-09-2

My Listening Ears

Joanne E. De Jonge

Illustrations by Rich Bishop

CONTENTS

MY LISTENING EARS

This is *not* a book about my ears. It's not about your ears either, or your eyes, nose, mouth, or any other part of your body that you probably figure you know.

Yet this *is* a book about your body. It's about the parts that you don't know. This book talks about eighteen feet of tubing curled up inside your belly and two million tubes hidden in your kidneys. It tells about glands which "talk" to each other, bones that eat themselves, and cells that eat germs. It tells you what is happening to that pizza you ate last night and why your knees shake when you're nervous. This book talks about your insides rather than your outsides.

So now you're probably wondering why this book isn't called something cute like *The Inside Story*. It is, after all, about insides and not ears. Why name it *My Listening Ears*? For two reasons.

First, this is a part of the series *My Father's World*. That title comes from the song "This Is My Father's World." So does this title about listening ears. It's a part of the song just as this book is a part of the series. And it does refer to at least one part of your body.

But this title also mentions listening; listening is important. That's the only way you're going to know what is going on inside of you.

Of course you can't listen in as your glands talk to each other. And you'll never hear a crunch as a bone eats itself. At most, you may hear your stomach rumble, but that doesn't tell you much.

Yet if you listen with your mind, you'll learn a lot. If you listen to people who have explored the body, you'll discover a fascinating world inside of your own skin.

The last part of this book doesn't talk about your body at all. It talks about Rose and rules and being squeezed into a mold. It tells about sad times and glad times. Mostly, it talks about people.

But if you listen closely, you'll hear that it is really talking about you. It's asking you to think about how you live, how other people treat you, and how you treat others.

Finally—and most importantly—if you listen with your heart, you'll know that this whole book is talking about you and God. It's telling you how God made you, his very special creature. And it's asking you to think about how you should live in your Father's world.

1

Living Bones

Where would you be without your bones? Probably nowhere. Or, at the most, you'd be a lump of skin and hair sprawled helplessly on the floor.

Imagine yourself a helpless mass of tissue, a shapeless glob on the floor. Now poke around through this mass of tissue—in your imagination. Poke carefully. Somewhere in there is your brain, protected only by skin and hair. One good jab at your brain would probably do you in.

Step back in your imagination and look at that mass. One lump is beating regularly—your heart, of course. Be careful! If someone should step on your heart, that would be the end of you!

Where are your lungs? Somewhere under that

mass of skin, your lungs are bravely trying to carry on. But it's tough going. They need to expand to take in air, and they're having trouble expanding all by themselves.

Enough of this nonsense. Have I made my point? Your bones do much more for you than you generally give them credit for. Of course, they enable you to stand, walk, run, and so on. But have you ever thought of how perfectly they are designed?

Take your skull, for example. The top of your skull has eight bones joined solidly so that they don't move. That's protection for your brain. If those bones were jointed and could move, you'd probably stand a chance of throwing your skull out of joint and injuring your brain.

Yet the bottom of your skull, your jaw, is movable. That's good. How would you eat or talk if you couldn't move your jaw?

Your ribs are entirely different from your skull. They're bones, but they must move so that you can breathe. So your ribs aren't joined solidly like the top of your skull. Instead, each rib is connected to your breastbone (the bone down your middle front) by elastic-like tissue. This makes the ribs flexible. Your rib cage can raise and lower so that your lungs can take in air and let it out.

Of course, your ribs also protect your heart and your lungs. If your ribs weren't there, one poke at your chest might hit you square in the heart. That could be fatal.

Now think about your backbone. That's a miracle of construction. It's made of thirty-three separate bones that look like spools of thread. Each "spool" is rigid, but the whole string of "spools" is flexible. If it weren't flexible, you'd walk like a wooden soldier. Try to sit in a chair once without moving your backbone.

Seven separate "spools" in your neck allow you to turn your head in almost every direction except completely around. Imagine what life would be like if you had to turn your whole body every time you wanted to turn your head. Try watching a tennis match with a stiff neck.

Between each of these "spools" in your backbone is a little cushion. That's protection for your brain. If you didn't have these cushions, your brain would be jolted every time you took a step.

Hold your arms out and twist them around. You can move your hands in almost any direction because the bottom half of each arm can twist almost completely around. That's because the two bones in that part of your arm are placed so that they can glide over each other. If you had only one bone there, or if the two bones were put together differently, you wouldn't be able to twist your arms. Try to pour a glass of milk and drink it without twisting your arms. You'll be glad that those two bones are joined as they are.

Not only are your bones placed just right to allow you to work, they also work for you. You see, bones aren't just hard, dead things that give you shape. They are very much alive.

Bone cells take food from your blood and give waste chemicals back to it, just like other living cells do. They store calcium and give it to your blood when other parts of your body need it. Bone marrow, the inside part of some bones, makes new red blood cells, enough to replace those cells every three or four months. If your bones were not alive, you wouldn't be alive.

Sometimes your bones seem almost to have minds of their own. When you break a bone, the cells seem to know exactly what to do. First, blood clots around the broken area. This stops the flow of blood from torn blood vessels. Then many more bone cells appear at the break. Some cells "eat" the pieces of injured bone. Other cells build new bone on the broken edges. Each edge of the break builds toward the other edge. Finally the edges meet, forming a strong bridge. When the bone is healed, the worker cells in that area stop building. The bone is complete again.

Of course, it helps to have a cast. That puts the broken pieces of bone in line so that the bone heals straight. But the real work of healing is done by the bone, not the cast.

Even if you don't break a bone, your bones are constantly breaking themselves down and re-building. Cells within your bones act as little destroyers and dissolve parts of the bone to release some chemicals. But you don't have to worry. Before the bone is really weakened, these same cells change jobs and become rebuilders. Gradually they lay down layers of fresh bone.

Right now, within your arms and legs and ribs, some of your bone cells are breaking down bones. Other cells are building up your bones. Some bones are making new red blood cells and others, possibly, are releasing chemicals into your blood. Your bones are alive and well.

Because they are alive and well, you are alive and well. You're much more than a lump of flesh sprawled helplessly on the floor—thanks to your bones. But of course, your bones are alive and well thanks to the One who made you.

2

The Trouble with George

"That's the trouble with George," she concluded. "He's spineless. He's got a wet noodle for a backbone."

She paused, half expecting me to agree with her opinion of "the trouble with George." I didn't.

I knew what she was trying to say. George, she thought, is a wishy-washy character. He doesn't voice his own opinions. In my opinion, however, she just doesn't listen closely to George's opinions. George is the soft-spoken type, and she's not a good listener. George certainly isn't spineless, and his backbone is *not* a wet noodle.

At least the last time I saw George his backbone was fine. He was sitting, standing, walking, and even moving his head. I didn't look at his back, but I assume his spine was still there. Otherwise he wouldn't have been doing all those things. George would have been a helpless lump of flesh without his spine. His whole body, from his legs up to his head, would have collapsed. George has his spine all right, and it's much more than a wet noodle. It's solid bone.

Well, not quite solid. George would be in bad shape if his backbone were solid. He wouldn't be able to bend, twist and turn, or even move his head.

George's backbone is actually a series of bone rings called vertebrae, linked together. It's held in place by straps of ligaments and a pair of large muscle masses. When George shakes his head, the top vertebrae move independently of the bottom ones. When he twists and turns his body, the middle vertebrae do the work. The bottom vertebrae are fused together, but George doesn't have a tail to wag, so he just has more support down there.

George does have a littly "jelly" in his spine;

but then, we all do. We'd probably be slightly loony without it. Between twenty-four of his vertebrae, George has little "jelly doughnuts" called discs. Each disc has a rather firm covering but is filled inside with soft, gelatin-like "jelly." These are George's shock absorbers.

When he walks, runs, or sits down hard, his body hits the pavement or the chair with a thud. Shock waves travel up his backbone. That "jelly" in his discs absorbs some of the shock. If those discs weren't in place, George's brain would rattle in his skull with every step he took. Any brain—even George's—can stand only so much banging. So, besides allowing George to move more freely, those discs also protect him when he moves.

I know that George doesn't always stand up straight. I suppose, like most of us, he should stand straighter for his own good. But actually his spine itself is slightly curved. It looks like a poorly printed S. The S-curve helps the discs absorb jolts when George walks. If his spine were straight as a flag pole, shock waves could travel more easily from bottom to top. Now they must slow down around the S-curve. The S-curve also protects George's backbone. It's easier to snap a straight pole than a curved one. George's spine is curved so that it won't break easily.

If George did break his back, he could really be in a peck of trouble, especially if he severed his spinal cord. This cord runs through George's vertebrae. It's only about three-quarters of an inch (2 cm) wide, seventeen inches (43 cm) long, and weighs a mere one and a half ounces (42 grams). Yet this bundle of nerves relays all the messages between George's brain and his other body parts. If he would sever his spinal cord, George would be paralyzed from the break down.

Utterly important, the spinal cord. That's why it's so well protected. It's wrapped in three layers of sheathing, bathed in a liquid shock absorber, and surrounded by bony vertebrae. Unless George has a serious accident, all will be well.

The last time I saw George, all was well. He was sitting, standing, walking—doing everything most people do. He was even voicing his own opinions. George certainly does have a backbone, and it's a lot more than a wet noodle.

"Well," she prompted me, "don't you think he's spineless?"

I wasn't about to trace my thoughts for her. Nor was I about to agree.

I simply said, "No."

Silently I said a little prayer of thanks for my own backbone—and for friends like George.

3

Muscles at Work

Where would you be without your muscles? Probably nowhere, because you can't move or do anything without muscles. In fact, you can't live without muscles.

We don't think about our muscles very often, although we use them all the time. Of course, some people work very hard to build up their muscles. But muscles that you can build up by exercise are only a small part of the muscles in your body. They just happen to be the muscles you think about the most.

Those muscles are called *skeletal* or *voluntary* muscles—"skeletal" because they're connected to your bones, or your skeleton; "voluntary" because you can control their actions voluntarily.

You can raise your hand, kick your foot, walk, swim, and do countless other things because you have skeletal muscles. You move when you want to because you can control these muscles.

But you have other muscles in your body that aren't connected to your bones. These muscles are called *involuntary* muscles. You can't control these muscles. To put it another way, you don't *have to* control these muscles. Because of the way God created you, those muscles work automatically. If you'd think about all the work these muscles do, you'd be glad that you don't have to control them.

One type of involuntary muscle is cardiac muscle. Your heart is made of cardiac muscle. Cardiac muscles work every minute you're alive. They contract, or squeeze together, to make the heart pump blood into your arteries. They relax to let blood rush into your heart.

Imagine how difficult life would be if your heart were a voluntary muscle. You would have to think about it every minute of your life. You would spend all your time thinking, "Squeeze. Relax. Squeeze. Relax." You wouldn't even be able to sleep.

Another type of involuntary muscle is called smooth muscle—"smooth" because it looks very smooth under a microscope.

Smooth muscles are found all over your body: in your blood vessels, in your kidneys, in your stomach, in your digestive tract, even in your eyelids. They regulate the flow of blood, push blood through your kidneys to be cleaned, churn your food, push it through your intestines, make you blink, and perform all sorts of other tasks.

Imagine what would happen if you had to think about regulating all these things. It would be hard to know just how big or small to make your arteries. If your blood flowed too close to the surface of your skin on a cold day, you'd probably nearly freeze the inside of your body. How would you know when to move your food from your stomach to your intestines? Could you remember to blink enough? If not, your eyeballs would dry up. Could you do all this and still remember to keep your heart beating? It's really a good thing that God made so many of our muscles involuntary.

Even our voluntary muscles are involuntary in a way. We can decide when and how to move them, but we don't have to think about *how* they work. That too is a good thing, because muscles are quite complicated.

Every muscle has millions of little parts called muscle cells. All the cells work together as a team.

Every muscle cell has hundreds of tiny fibers laid side by side. Thin fibers, called actin, lay next to thick fibers, called myosin. The myosin fibers have little hooks on them that can reach out and hitch into the actin fibers. Then the myosin fibers contract and pull the actin fibers with them.

When a muscle contracts, all the cells don't

contract at the same time. Each cell can contract for only a fraction of a second. So some cells in a muscle contract while others relax. Then the relaxed cells contract and the others rest. The cells are coordinated so that they contract and relax in shifts the whole time the muscle is working. Since each cell contracts for only a fraction of a second, you can imagine how much work is going on in that muscle in just one minute.

Muscles don't contract unless nerves tell them to. This "telling" is a very complicated process, involving both chemical and electrical reactions that all happen in a fraction of a second. It's very hard to understand, so it would be nearly impossible to control.

Can you imagine what would happen if you had to control all the messages that shot through your muscles? It takes much more time to think about it than it does for the messages to be sent. It would be impossible to keep the chemical formulas and electrical messages straight.

How would you know just which cells to contract? Could you remember to give them a rest every second and contract other cells? Could you coordinate two muscles in your toe or all your leg muscles? Could you take one step and still keep your blood flowing and your heart beating? Don't forget to blink—both eyes!

God knew that we wouldn't be able to keep that all straight. That's why he made muscles the way he did. Aren't you glad?

4

More Trouble with George

"That's really the trouble with George," she concluded. "The guy doesn't have any nerve."

I sighed, remembering the last time she had diagnosed George's "trouble." Then she had reduced him to a quivering, formless mass by giving him a wet noodle instead of a backbone. This time she even took away the quivers. She said he had no nerves.

"Of course George has nerves," I wanted to shout. "He quivers, doesn't he?" George's nerves are what makes his muscles move, down to the very last quiver. A nerve must send a "move" message to a muscle before that muscle will do a thing. If George so much as quivers, he's got at least one nerve.

Of course George has nerves. He has more than 10 billion of them! At last count, George had about 3 thousand nerves connecting his taste buds to his brain, 100 thousand nerve cells lodged in his ears, and 130 million light-receiving nerve cells in his eyes. His skin was a blanket of nerves: 30 thousand heat receptors, 250 thousand cold sensors, and nearly 500 thousand touch spots covered his skin.

These are just *some* of his sensory nerves. They're the nerves that help George sense the world about him. They bring messages from the outside world to George's brain. I've seen George react to these messages. He's commented on the smell and taste of a steak. He's enjoyed a beautiful sunset, and he's put on a sweater in a cold room.

George couldn't react without his motor nerves. When George's brain thinks, "It's cold; put on a sweater," nerves in one of his arms fire on those muscles. George's arm reaches out and picks up his sweater. George couldn't move if he didn't have motor nerves to fire on his muscles. Actually, those nerves don't build an actual fire, like a bonfire. Rather, they work electrically. A tiny current travels down each nerve, boosted on its way by a chemical relay station at the nerve's end.

Each nerve looks somewhat like a pollywog. The nerve cell is the pollywog's body. A nerve fiber runs from the cell, like the pollywog's tail. The electrical current, or impulse, travels down that fiber.

Some of George's nerves relay messages

quickly. The impulse can travel 325 miles (523 km) an hour. That takes only a split second inside of his body. Other messages may "creep" along at 1½ miles (2.4 km) per hour. That's why, when George cuts his finger, he knows it a split second before he feels the pain—the pressure message travels more quickly than the pain message.

But George is OK. His nerves are working fine. In fact, some work so well that he doesn't even think about them. What happens when George touches a hot stove? He pulls his hand away before he thinks about it. Heat-sensing nerves in his hand tell muscle-firing nerves in the same hand to move. They don't even consult his brain first. They simply act for George's protection.

Or take the way George blinks when something flies in his face. That's another reflex action, one which doesn't ask the brain for permission first.

George has good reflexes. He coughs when a piece of food goes down the wrong tube. He waves his arms when he stumbles, to avoid falling. There's nothing wrong with George's nerves! In fact, George has a whole division of his nervous system designed to work without his telling it to. That's what keeps him breathing, helps him digest his food, and keeps his heart beating. All those activities take muscles, you know. His nerves must tell those muscles to work, so the autonomic division of his nervous system keeps right on firing on those muscles, whether or not George thinks about it.

George doesn't usually think about his heart-beat or digestion. He figures he has better things to think about, like the sunset or the taste of that steak. And no matter what George thinks about, he uses thousands, maybe millions, of nerve cells to think. His brain is all nerve cells, billions of them, with more connections than anyone can count. Of course George's brain works all the time—even when he's asleep—so those nerves work constantly.

And while he sleeps, his brain sends messages down his spinal cord to all parts of his body to tell them what to do. And those parts send messages back, telling his brain about the world around him. Even while he sleeps, his nerves are alert and active. George wouldn't last very long without his nerves.

"Well, don't you agree?" she prodded me.

I sighed once more. Again, I wasn't about to trace my thoughts for her. But I also wasn't about to agree with her.

Once more I said a little prayer—this time in thanks for my own nerves. And maybe asking for a little more nerve.

"No, I don't agree," I said softly. "George has nerve. He quivers, doesn't he?"

I don't think she understood.

5

Apples, Asparagus, and Clams

Last Sunday our minister happened to quote the old saying "You are what you eat." Immediately my mind began to wander, and I pictured myself made up of exactly what I eat most.

My head was a big juicy orange with jelly beans for eyes, a roll of Certs for teeth, a raw carrot in place of a nose, and two big apples where ears should be. My arms were corncobs, my legs were stalks of asparagus, and fried clams took the place of fingers and toes. Coursing through my veins was strong black coffee, my lungs were cheeseburgers with olives and mayonnaise, and my heart was one large mushroom pizza.

All these foods do really become part of us, but we'd never recognize them in their final form.

Usually we enjoy the taste of good food, chew it, swallow it, and forget it. If digestion were up to us, most of our food would probably stay in our stomachs just the way we swallowed it.

Maybe that's why God made our digestive systems so automatic. Maybe he knew that we'd love to eat but wouldn't have the patience or the ability to take care of digesting our foods, so he made digestion able to take care of itself.

You know what it's like to drool at the sight or smell of a good meal. That's simply the result of saliva glands pouring saliva into your mouth to wet the food so that you can swallow it. Saliva also makes it possible for you to taste food, because dry food has no real taste. Although you have no control of the situation, saliva also starts digestion by changing anything starchy that you eat, like bread, to a simple sugar your body can use.

Once you swallow, the food is beyond your control. In fact, even *when* you swallow, the opening to your windpipe closes automatically so that your food will go down the right tube. If food goes down your windpipe, you automatically cough to get rid of it.

Within your stomach there are about 35 million glands that produce almost two and one-half quarts of digestive juice a day. When food enters your stomach, your stomach automatically begins churning and producing these juices to help break down the food. Digestive juice is so powerful that it could severely burn any other part of your body. This juice breaks down any kind of food in your stomach, yet it doesn't break down the stomach itself.

One of the juices produced by the stomach glands is called gastrin. It flows directly into the bloodstream and signals the stomach to make gastric juices. If there is a lot of gastric juice in the stomach, the glands will produce less gastrin. And this in turn will cause a slowdown in the production of gastric juices. This kind of control keeps the whole digestive system in balance.

Three to five hours after you have swallowed and forgotten your food, it has been broken down to a liquid form by strong gastric juices. Then it passes into your small intestine. Strong muscles automatically push it through the twenty feet of your small intestine. This intestine is covered inside by about five million hair-like pieces of flesh, called villi. These villi carry blood vessels very close to their surfaces. As the liquid food passes over the villi, some of it is absorbed into the blood in the blood vessels and carried to different parts of your body.

Glands in your pancreas and liver pour digestive fluids into your small intestine to help break down the food further.

While this digestion is taking place, muscles keep pushing the food forward automatically. Muscles between the intestines, called sphincter muscles, keep the food moving in the right direction slowly enough for digestion to take place.

If you eat breakfast at 7 AM, that food passes from your small intestine to your large intestine sometime between 1 PM and 9 PM the same day, long after you've forgotten it. Much of the nourishment has passed into your bloodstream.

The process of digestion is completed in your large intestine. No more juices are added. In fact, juices are usually taken away, and anything that your body can't use is concentrated into one mass for disposal.

The whole process of digestion is longer and more complicated than we usually imagine. What a chore it would be if we had to consciously digest all our food! Can you even remember what you ate twelve hours ago? Yet God constructed our bodies to work so automatically and efficiently that even when we don't think about it, our muscles are still churning our food, absorbing the nourishment, and concentrating the waste. I'm afraid that if I had to do the work consciously, my ears would really be apples, my legs asparagus, and my fingers clams.

6

Amazing Tubing

Pat your stomach.

You probably patted your belly, below your waistline and between your hip bones, right? That's not your stomach; that's your intestines. Your stomach is higher.

Lots of people make that mistake. That's because lots of people think about their stomachs, but hardly anyone thinks about his or her intestines. That's all right, because your intestines were created to work all by themselves. You really don't have to think about them. But if you look sometime to find out about them, you'll discover that you have some amazing tubing there.

By the time you are full-grown, you'll have over twenty-five feet of intestines coiled within your body. Imagine four full-sized adult men lying in a row, head to foot. Now, in your imagination, take a rubber hose and stretch it the full length of this row. Now think about curling up that hose and fitting it into your belly. Quite a trick, isn't it? Yet that's how much tubing most adults have neatly coiled inside of them.

Of course, it isn't rubber tubing. It's much more complicated than that. It's living tissue, designed to help you digest your food.

Before your food is digested, it must be broken into pieces so small you could only see them under a microscope. Your stomach starts the work, but your small intestine does the main job. Food

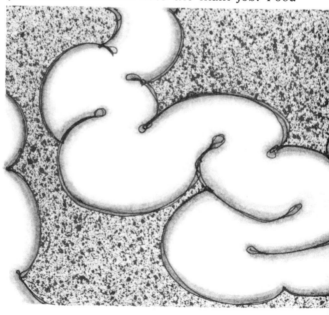

doesn't break down all by itself. It needs some help from certain proteins, called enzymes, that work to break down the food. So within your small intestine lie glands that produce these enzymes. Not five or ten glands, not even hundreds. You have about *180 million* glands lining your small intestine. Each gland is created to produce the proper enzyme at the proper time.

After your food is broken down, the nourishment must be picked up by your blood. Broken-down food does you no good if it stays in your intestine. So you have a special system to move the food from your small intestine to your blood.

That system is based right where the food is—

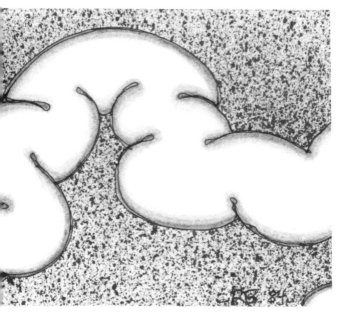

inside your small intestine. The inside of this intestine isn't smooth, like the inside of a rubber hose. Instead, it's filled with extremely tiny "fingers" called villi. They're part of the inside "skin" and they reach into your intestine. Each villus, or "finger," has a blood vessel running through it. So blood vessels are reaching right into your intestine to pick up food. These blood vessels are connected to others that bring that food-rich blood to all parts of your body.

Now, that doesn't sound especially amazing until you think about it a bit. It really is just the right way to bring lots of blood near lots of food in a little bit of space. One little experiment will help you understand.

Hold up your left hand and make a fist. Take a string and measure the distance over your knuckles. Now open your fist and spread your fingers. Take a string and measure the distance up and down all of your fingers. You've used a lot more string, haven't you? That's what the inside of your small intestine is like. Many more blood vessels can reach in because your villi are there.

But your villi aren't as big as fingers. If they were, you'd be able to fit only about ten into your intestine. Instead, they're so tiny you can't see them without a microscope. So you don't have ten or even twenty villi. You have so many that no one has ever counted them. Scientists think that most intestines have about *five million* villi within them!

More amazing yet, each of those five million

villi have smaller "fingers" called microvilli. Within your small intestine you have more microvilli than you can imagine.

All of this, of course, gives your body a large area from which to absorb food. If you would spread a rubber hose the size of your small intestine out on a floor, it would cover about one-third the space taken by a single bed, about six square feet. But if you would spread out this intestine, including all the villi and microvilli, so that all the bumps on its surface were lying flat, you'd cover about ninety square feet, the size of a small bedroom. All that area, neatly coiled inside your body, helps you digest food.

Digesting food is really a complicated process. Your body can't take a small bit of pizza and expect your blood to use it. It can't transport last night's meatloaf directly to your muscles for energy. All of that food must be broken down to simple bits that your body can use. Your small intestine does most of that work.

When food hits your small intestine, it's a liquid "soup" called chyme. It's full of acid from your stomach, but it isn't nearly ready for your blood. First your intestine must take care of the acid. Some of its 180 million glands produce a substance called secretin. This is sent through the blood vessels to an organ called your pancreas. Your pancreas "sees" secretin in your blood and immediately makes an anti-acid juice that pours directly into your intestine. Somehow your pancreas "knows" just how much anti-acid to make. It always sends just enough to take care of the acid.

But the food still isn't broken down enough. So, as we mentioned earlier, your intestine produces enzymes to break down some foods. And it produces another substance that mixes with some liquid from your pancreas to break down proteins. It also produces another substance that "tells" your gall bladder to send something to help digest fats. And on and on and on.

It's all very complicated, yet somehow it all works perfectly. By the time your food is pushed to the end of your small intestine, most of the nourishment has been absorbed by your blood.

Did you notice that I have been saying "small intestine"? The twenty-five feet of tubing is your small and large intestines together. But all of the glands and villi we have been talking about are found in your small intestine, which is less than twenty-five feet. All that complicated work is done by your small intestine. Your large intestine has another job. But that's another story.

By now you may be aware that your small intestine is much more important than you thought. It really does the work of digesting your food. Without your small intestine you would starve. No other part of your body—not even your stomach—can do this important job.

Yet you probably don't think about your small intestine very often. You don't have to, because it was designed to work just right on its own. But sometime you may think to thank the Designer for such a gift.

7

Hearts and Valentines

Once each year comes Valentine's Day, and on this special day classrooms and mailboxes will be aflutter with paper hearts and messages: "Be my valentine" or "You're my valentine." In all this flurry and fuss, not many of us wonder how the custom originated.

Long ago, the Romans set aside February 14 as a day devoted to love lotteries. It was also on February 14, A.D. 270, that a young martyr named St. Valentine was killed for refusing to give up his Christianity. According to legend, he left a farewell letter for the jailer's daughter and signed it "From your Valentine." These two occurrences have become mingled into the one happy day of paper hearts that we call Valentine's Day.

Everyone knows why we use hearts: the heart is supposed to be the very center of our emotions. We say that someone talking sincerely is talking "from the heart." We refer to people as being "good-hearted." The heartbeat stands for the very life of a person, and well it might. Without our hearts and their continuous beating, we couldn't live.

This muscular pump is only about the size of a clenched fist and weighs less than a pound. Yet it is responsible for moving all the blood in the body, passing it through the lungs to pick up oxygen, and then recirculating it through the body.

The pumping action of the heart is timed so perfectly that the two top chambers receive blood from the body and from the lungs at exactly the same time, and pass it on to the lower chambers exactly together. The lower chambers, in perfect timing, squeeze the blood out to the lungs and to the body.

The heart is so sensitive that when a call for more oxygen-rich blood comes, it automatically beats faster.

The heart is so strong that, should you open the aorta (the main blood vessel leading away from the heart), blood would spurt up in a column six feet high. Day and night your little pump works on, pumping seventy to seventy-five times a minute when you are at rest. Five quarts of blood flow through your heart every minute while you are resting, and up to thirty-five quarts a minute while you are exercising.

From your heart the blood flows out to the farthest reaches of your body along 60,000 miles of tubing. It makes the complete trip from heart to farthest capillary back to the heart in twenty seconds. If some dye was put into your blood at your heart, within twenty seconds it would spread through your whole body—your muscles, your organs, your brain—no part would escape.

It's no wonder that hearts are used on Valentine's Day; they represent life itself.

In the Bible there are references to the heart that make me shudder. Jesus said, "Out of the heart come evil thoughts." That must mean that evil permeates every part of a man. When God said that "it grieved him to his heart" that he had made people, I imagine that God was sorry through every part of his being that he had created us.

But then it surely is reassuring to read, "The Lord set his heart in love upon your fathers . . . and chose their descendants after them." If we are God's people and he has set his heart in love on us, every part of him must be filled with love for us.

8

Lymph Lumps

Winter's coming, cold and flu season. Get ready to fight those germs!

In a way, your body *is* ready. You have a whole system, called your lymphatic system, designed to help keep you healthy.

When you get a cold, do you ever get swollen "glands"? You can feel little swollen lumps on your neck behind your ears, or under your arms. Those lumps are a part of that system. They swell when they're working hard to keep you from becoming ill.

Actually, those lumps aren't glands. Glands make small amounts of liquid. Sweat glands make sweat; salivary glands make saliva. Those lumps don't make a liquid. Strictly speaking, they're called nodes, lymph nodes. A node is a lump. So you really have swollen lumps, or swollen lymph lumps.

Don't let those ridiculous names make you think that they're ridiculous lumps. Lymph nodes (a better term than lymph lumps) are there for a purpose. They help fight infection.

When harmful bacteria and germs enter your bloodstream, some find their way to your lymph nodes. (You'll find out later how this happens.) As soon as your lymph nodes recognize harmful bacteria, cells in those nodes go to work. They produce germ-fighters called antibodies. These antibodies either destroy the bacteria completely or change them so that they aren't harmful to you. Other cells there, called macrophages, even eat some of the bacteria.

How lymph nodes recognize harmful bacteria and germs is a mystery to us. Somehow they work to destroy only those which are harmful. They let the good guys go.

Lymph nodes are scattered all over your body. You feel the nodes in your neck and under your arms because they're close to your skin. Most of your nodes are in your trunk, the main part of your body. They help clean blood which flows past your important organs. But you also have lymph nodes near your elbows and behind your knees.

There's more to your lymphatic system than nodes. It contains a whole system of vessels, much like your blood vessels, connecting your

nodes. This system actually works closely with your blood system, which contains two types of vessels: arteries (which carry blood from your heart to other body parts) and veins (which carry blood back to your heart).

When your blood carries food to your body cells, some liquid from your blood actually leaves your arteries. This liquid oozes around each cell to pass food directly to the cell. Then it returns to your blood through tiny veins. But some of the liquid can't squeeze into the veins. The molecules in the liquid are too big to get through the tiny holes in the vein walls. So that liquid is stranded around your cells. Then it's called lymph.

That's where your lymphatic system gets into the picture. Tiny tubes, called lymph vessels, lie close to the tiny veins. Liquids which can't pass into the veins can squeeze into lymph vessels.

These lymph vessels are connected to larger tubes, which are connected to larger tubes and to still larger tubes. So the lymph that the tiny vessels have picked up can flow through these tubes, away from the cells. Lymph nodes lie at certain points along these tubes. That's where the harmful germs and bacteria are singled out and destroyed.

The nodes aren't dead end. Lymph flows *through* the nodes, not just into them. Clean lymph flows out of them. The large lymph tubes connect with two veins in your chest. There the fluid that your blood lost at the body cells is returned to your blood.

So your lymphatic system helps to keep your blood free of harmful bacteria and germs. In that way it helps keep you healthy. But it does even more.

When you eat fatty foods, your blood can't absorb all of those big fat molecules. So lymph vessels near your intestines absorb them instead. They pass them into your blood at the point where your lymph enters your bloodstream.

Also, your lymph nodes produce certain cells called lymphocytes that travel into your blood. There they "look for" and destroy harmful bacteria. They act as an extra protection system to find and destroy the "bad guys" that have avoided your lymph nodes.

So if you feel a cold coming on, run your fingers down your neck. You may be able to feel your lymph nodes in action. But don't say that you have swollen glands. You know now that they're not glands. Just smile and say that you have swollen lymph lumps. They're helping you fight a battle. And because they're there, you'll probably win.

9

The Guardians Within

At this very moment hundreds, perhaps thousands, of invisible forces are trying to attack your body. Throughout this day—and every day of your life—billions of these forces will try to invade your body and harm you.

There's nothing mysterious about these forces. They're germs. They're so tiny you can't see them. There are so many of them that they attack in huge numbers.

They float in the air you breathe, they swim in the water you drink, they live in the food you eat. Some hitchike on bits of dust which land in your nose or eyes. Others cling to that pin which pricks your finger.

If certain germs entered your body and were

allowed to multiply unchecked, you could quickly die. One germ could become two in about twenty minutes. Those two could become a million within seven hours. The million could become several quadrillion within a day. Your body would be overwhelmed by germs.

Yet, even with these bleak prospects, you need not worry. Your body will fight the germs. It will successfully turn back most of the attacks of these countless invaders. You won't even know of the many battles taking place, because you have such a wonderful system of guardians within your body.

A speck of dust blows into your eye. Tears flow to wash out the dust. Soon the bothersome speck disappears and you forget the incident.

But several hundred germs hitchiked into your eye on that dust. You didn't feel them, but they were there. Your tears have also killed those germs.

In those tears washing over your eye is a strong germ-killer called lysozyme. It's so powerful that one tear dropped into a half gallon of water can still kill germs. You needn't worry too much about germs in your eyes.

If a germ rides on some dust into your nose, your body will react immediately. Your nose will tickle and you will sneeze out dust and germs. Or your nose will become irritated and drip, flushing out the dust and germs. If the germs remain after the dust leaves, lysozyme in the mucous of your nose will usually kill them.

If dust finds its way to the back of your nose and to the tubes below, you'll cough it out. Or it will become trapped in fluids. Again, lysozyme will kill the germs. Or you may swallow the dust. Then those germs must deal with the juices within your stomach, which are so powerful that almost no germ can survive.

Germs often enter your body through the food you eat. That's why your saliva contains an anti-septic which can kill harmful germs. Anything not killed by saliva will meet its fate in your stomach and intestines.

Suppose a germ tries to enter your body through a cut in your skin. It must survive life on your skin before it can find the cut. Even this is difficult, since your skin produces a layer of oils and water designed to trap germs and kill them. Some germs which can survive for hours in a drop of water will die within twenty minutes on the palm of your hand.

Sometimes germs do survive battles with your first line of guardians. Still, they don't automatically live and grow. They must fight several more lines of defense.

Imagine that you have stepped on a dirty nail. This is what happens.

Injured body cells near the wound release chemicals which travel away from the wound until they reach the nearest blood vessels. They cause the walls of the blood vessels to relax, allowing fluids to seep out of your blood vessels. Within these fluids are chemicals that stop the growth of bacteria. They surround the wound to kill the germs the nail left in your skin.

Certain white blood cells, called leukocytes, also seep out of those blood vessels. These cells are attracted to the wound like metal to a magnet. They "look for" germs which have entered your skin. Each leukocyte will find a germ, back it up against a solid surface, and "eat" it. Then the leukocyte will slither off in search of more germs. Millions of leukocytes rush to the scene of any infection.

A part of your blood called fibrinogen also seeps out of your blood vessels. When fibrinogen contacts air, it becomes a network of stick strands. With other substances it forms a wall

around the wound. This wall keeps the germs in one place.

If germs escape the wound and are free to wander within your body, still more guardians within you react. For example, chemicals released into your bloodstream will call extra fighting leukocytes from their storehouses. They will also alert your bone marrow to make more leukocytes.

Leukocytes can gobble up germs any place in your body. If they are killed by germs they can't overcome, they release chemicals which harm the germs.

If leukocytes can't take care of the germs, other blood cells, called macrophages, are marshalled into action. They're bigger than leukocytes and can destroy larger germs.

After leukocytes and macrophages have gobbled germs, your body still tries to make sure that those germs won't reach your bloodstream. Fluid containing these dead germs is run through your lymph nodes, which filter out the dead material. This is the final barrier which prevents germs from entering your bloodstream.

If germs do reach your bloodstream, several organs join the fight. Your bone marrow, liver, spleen, and several smaller organs contain millions of microphages (a smaller version of macrophages). As your blood passes through these organs, the microphages gobble up germs. Also, your body manufactures antibodies, little bits which can fight off viruses and other unwelcome guests.

Most of the time germs do not make it that far into your body. Considering the number of germs that try—billions every day—very few are successful. Surprisingly few. In fact, some people who study germs are surprised by how healthy we remain. They say that, because we have so many germs attacking us daily, how we can remain healthy is a mystery.

I don't think it's a mystery. I think it's because we have such wonderful guardians, placed within us by our Supreme Guardian.

10

A Journey into Your Lungs

I'm going for a ride on a very special balloon.
I'll be floating between "trees," through "tunnels," and into huge rooms. I'll even take a side
trip on a boat before I float back home. Would
you like to come along?

You'll have to imagine yourself very tiny; the
balloon on which we'll ride is one molecule of
oxygen. The trip we'll take is through a person's
respiratory, or breathing, system. Ready? Here
we go!

We're floating around in the air, so tiny that no
one can see us. Suddenly, we're caught in a gust
of wind and pulled close to a huge "cave." Someone is breathing us in.

Look at the cave entrance. Huge "trees" stand

guard. They're really bristly little hairs. They act as a screen to keep dust particles from rushing far into the nose. But we're much smaller than dust particles, so we go swooshing into the cave-nose, between the tree-hairs.

The far end of the cave looks narrow, and the walls are covered with something soft and sticky. That's mucus. If the hairs didn't stop dirt in the air, the mucus will. Lungs shouldn't have even the smallest bit of dirt in them.

Now we've gone through the nose and around a bend; we find ourselves in a huge tunnel. This is the pharynx. If you look straight down you can see a division in the tunnel. Beneath us is a long, open passage that leads to the stomach. Another passage, branching off, is guarded by a trap door. That's the route we want to take.

That little trap door is called the epiglottis. It almost seems to have a mind of its own, because it works without a person even thinking about it.

When you breathe, your epiglottis remains open so that air can travel to your lungs. When you swallow food or water, the epiglottis clamps down and shuts off the air passage. The only open route is to your stomach, where food and water should go. If this didn't happen, you would quickly choke on your food. Have you ever tried to breathe and swallow at the same time? You stop breathing when you swallow, because your epiglottis has closed your air passage.

This epiglottis is open right now, and we fly into a wide room. It has two tough elastic bands stretched over the far entry way. That's funny—the bands wiggle, vibrating every time air comes through them. We're in the voice box, or larynx. Those two "elastic bands" are vocal cords. Their vibrations make the sound waves of a person's speech.

Let's continue our journey. Through the larynx we go, into a long, wide tube that has tough elastic rings around it. This is the trachea, the main air tube. Those rings keep it from collapsing.

If you look down, you'll see that the trachea divides into two smaller passages also ringed with "elastic." These are called bronchi; one leads into the left lung and one leads into the right.

Suddenly we're whooshed through one of the bronchi, around a corner into a smaller passage, then a still smaller one and into an even smaller tunnel. Each bronchus branches again and again into thousands of tiny tunnels called bronchioles.

Look at the end of the bronchiole we're in. There's a whole cluster of balloon-like sacs, like a bunch of grapes. The walls of these sacs are super-thin. There's blood rushing through thin tubes around the outside of each sac.

Right now the sacs are much bigger than we are, because we're as small as an oxygen molecule. Actually, these sacs, or alveoli, are tiny and bunched together. You have about 300,000,000 *separate* alveoli in your lungs. If you could take all the thin tissue from your alveoli and spread it out, it would about cover a badminton court. That's a lot of tissue folded around inside your lungs.

Blood picks up oxygen through the thin walls of the alveoli. That's why you can see it rushing around out there. Because you have so much tissue in your alveoli with so much blood circulating around it, your body can get all the oxygen it needs.

Back to our trip. Let's whoosh into one alveolus.

Look at the walls of the little room and you'll see a lot of activity. We're so small that these tissue-thin walls look like chicken wire. The river of blood rushing past the outside is actually made of little solid things bumping against each other. Some of these look like ferryboats, carrying passengers. Those passengers bump off into the alveolus, and new passengers squeeze through the "chicken wire" to get on.

The "ferryboats" are really red blood cells, scooped out in the middle like little lifeboats. The "passengers" that get off are carbon dioxide molecules, which the body doesn't need. Incoming passengers are oxygen molecules, which the body can use.

Since we're hooked to an oxygen molecule, it's time for our boat ride. Squeeze through the "chicken wire," hop on a "ferryboat," and away we go.

What a trip it is! With blinding speed we rush

from the little tube through bigger and bigger tubes. We pause a split second in a huge room, a chamber in the heart, and then are squeezed out. On we rush through smaller and smaller tubes. Gradually we slow down a bit and finally come to rest in a tiny tube beside a large, busy "factory."

This "factory" is one of the trillions of cells in the body. It needs oxygen for all the work it does. While it works it makes carbon dioxide, which it cannot use.

If you look closely, you can see the cell unloading carbon dioxide into the ferryboats and picking up oxygen.

Wait a minute! We may be as small as an oxygen molecule right now, but we don't want to get caught in the cell's machinery! This looks like the end of the line. It is the end of the line for the oxygen. That little molecule is right where it's needed.

This shouldn't be the end of the line for us, though. Let's imagine ourselves back the way we came. Through the heart, back to the lungs, into the alveoli, bronchioles, bronchi, trachea, larynx, and pharynx, past the epiglottis, through the nose, to normal size. Finally, we have our normal bodies back!

Did you ever realize that your "normal" body included such complicated tunnels and passageways? Can you imagine that, every time you breathe, millions of oxygen molecules take that trip that we just took? Each molecule goes exactly where it's needed when it's needed, and you never even think about it. If you had to direct each molecule, you'd really be in trouble. You'd never be able to do it. You wouldn't ever be able to keep track of it all.

Maybe that's why God made our complicated breathing systems as perfect and as automatic as he did.

11

Two Million Tiny Tubes

Within each one of us rests two special little organs. They're not very big. The two of them placed end to end on this book would extend only about two inches beyond the bottom of this page. Yet they are so important that without them we would die. They help our bodies clean waste materials from our blood. They're called kidneys.

Kidneys may be small, but they're not simple. They're packed with hundreds of thousands of blood vessels and tubes. Their work is so complicated that we can hardly understand exactly how it's done. The most we can do is follow the path of blood through a kidney and try to discover what happens.

When blood is pumped into a kidney, it follows

a very definite pathway. Very specific things happen along this pathway.

First, the blood is pumped into a tiny tangle of blood vessels called a glomerulus. It looks like a bit of fluffy cotton and is surrounded by a cap. The cap is called a Bowman's capsule. When the blood is in the glomerulus, water and some chemicals from the blood leak through the walls and are collected in the capsule. So the blood flowing out of the glomerulus is much thicker than the blood flowing in because it has lost so much water.

Next, the thickened blood flows through a blood vessel that's wrapped around a twisted, looped tube. This tube is connected to the Bowman's capsule, so the water and chemicals that left the blood are flowing through it.

At this point there are two sets of tubes twisted and looped around each other. One carries thick blood, the other carries water and chemicals. The blood needs to get back some of the water or it will be too thick when it leaves the kidneys. It may also need some of the chemicals that were pushed into the Bowman's capsule.

Somehow, within these twists and turns, all the necessary exchanges take place. Sodium ions, which the body needs, are pumped into the blood. Chlorine ions filter back in. Water filters back in. Ammonia, which is harmful to the body, has been changed into urea. Urea stays in the tubes and doesn't go back into the blood.

If the amount of some substance in the blood

is unusually high, the tubes will absorb a bit of it. If the amount of another substance is low, the blood will absorb it again. This happens automatically. A person never has to think of what the blood needs and doesn't need. All of that happens perfectly. A very delicate balance is kept in the blood so that the temperature and chemical balances inside the body will remain the same, as much as possible.

After the blood has gone through all these twists and turns, it's back to normal. It has the right amount of water and everything else in it. All that's missing are the harmful waste products. The clean blood leaves the kidney through a vein and is on its way to the rest of the body.

The waste material and a little bit of water pass from the tube into a collecting sac called the bladder. From there it passes out of the body as urine.

All these twisting and turning tubes do have a name. Each set of tubes, together with the glomerulus and the Bowman's capsule, is called a nephron. Nephrons are only about half an inch long. The tubes are so tiny that you cannot see them without a microscope. Each kidney contains about one million nephrons. So we have about two million tiny tubes within our bodies, working automatically to keep our blood just right.

Every minute, more than one quart of blood is pumped through a person's kidneys through two million nephrons. Your kidneys clean all of the blood in your body (almost five and one-half quarts) about once every five minutes.

Think for a minute about what would happen if your kidneys didn't work just right.

Suppose blood didn't absorb water back from the tubes. You would lose hundreds of pounds of water every day. You would have to drink over a hundred quarts of water every day, just to keep your blood thin enough.

Suppose the tubes didn't take extra substances from the blood. Those things would build up in your blood and throw all your body systems off balance.

Suppose the tubes didn't keep urea, but let it filter back into the blood. Harmful ammonia would spread throughout your body and poison you.

But you don't have to suppose. Usually kidneys work just right. Every minute that you're alive, two million nephrons work automatically to keep you healthy. And you never even think about it.

"I praise you because I am fearfully and wonderfully made" (Ps. 139:14).

12

Four Little "Peas"

A woman I know had an operation recently. She had her parathyroid glands removed, I heard. At least, some of them were removed. I was told that the doctors put one gland back, but they put it into her arm instead of back into her neck, where it came from. That way if something goes wrong with it, it's easier to get at.

When I first heard about the surgery, I thought it was really strange. Usually we don't rearrange our body parts like that and expect everything to work right. When doctors take out an appendix or tonsils, they usually take them all the way out. They don't sew them up into an arm or a leg. Why did they move this gland? Why didn't they simply remove it? How could they expect it to work in an arm instead of a neck?

I wasn't questioning the doctors. They must have known what they were doing when they put the gland into the arm. But *I* didn't know, and I was curious. So I did a little reading and discovered some amazing facts about the way our bodies work.

First, parathyroid glands are pea-sized glands found in your neck. They're called parathyroid because they're on your thyroid gland. *Para* means "beside," so they're your "beside the thyroid" glands.

Parathyroid glands are part of your endocrine gland system. *Endo* means "within." Your endocrine glands pour their hormones (the juices they make) directly into your bloodstream.

Other glands in your body send hormones down tubes into certain places. Tear glands send tears to your eyes. Glands in your stomach make digestive juices. Those glands, tubes, and ducts can't be moved. You wouldn't want to digest your eyeballs or shed tears into your stomach.

Doctors can move a parathyroid gland because it is an endocrine gland. Its hormones go to all parts of the body. If they begin their journey in an arm instead of a neck, it really doesn't matter.

There are four parathyroid glands; we think that they all work alike. That's why doctors can remove some of the glands. They have to leave at least one gland. A person would die without the hormone from those tiny glands.

That particular hormone is called parathor-

mone because it's a *para*thyroid *hormone*. Parathormone controls the amount of calcium found
in your blood and your body cells. It helps your
intestines absorb calcium from the food passing
through them. It helps your kidneys absorb calcium from your urine, and it helps bone cells
give up calcium stored in them.

We don't know exactly how this works. We just
know that, without parathormone, your intestines and your kidneys wouldn't keep enough
calcium in your blood. And your bones wouldn't
release enough calcium.

Your muscles and nerves need calcium to work
properly. With too little calcium, nerve cells become overactive. They send too many messages
to muscle cells, and the muscles can go into
spasms. A person can have convulsions and die
from lack of calcium in the blood.

You also shouldn't have too *much* calcium in
your blood. That's as harmful as not enough.
Your brain cells and heart cells are sensitive to
calcium. A person with too much calcium may
become mentally disturbed. A heart that receives
too much calcium may simply stop beating. Also,
if your bones give up too much calcium, they
become soft and begin to break.

So the amount of calcium in your blood is very
important. Too much or too little can be fatal. A
very delicate balance must be kept. That's the
work of the parathyroid glands.

The story doesn't end with your parathyroid
glands pouring their hormone into your blood.

They must pour just the right amount, since too much parathormone keeps too much calcium in the blood. Your parathyroid glands can't work alone. Something must tell them how much parathormone to make.

That "something" is your blood. If you have plenty of calcium in your blood, your parathyroid glands receive a message: "Cut down on the parathormone. There's enough calcium here." So less hormone flows, bones give up less calcium, intestines and kidneys absorb less, and you're fine.

If your blood needs more calcium, your glands receive another message: "Help. Calcium needed." Your parathyroid pours more parathormones into your blood. That makes bones give up more calcium, and intestines and kidneys absorb more. Your calcium level goes up until it reaches the right level.

If the level keeps going up, your gland gets another message: "Stop. We have enough." And the hormone level goes back down.

Usually, when we talk about the wonder of our bodies, we mention our eyes or our hearts or our nerves. I've never heard anyone talk about the wonder of our parathyroid glands. Maybe they're too small to be noticed often. Or maybe, because they work so well, we don't think about them often.

I suppose that's also true about other parts of our bodies. They work so smoothly and cooperate so well that we don't notice them. Only when we sit down and think about it do we realize how amazing our bodies really are.

Now I have a confession to make. When I started reading about the parathyroid glands, I thought that I'd find out about all the endocrine glands. But I became so involved with understanding the parathyroids that I haven't gotten to the others yet.

There are other endocrine glands, you know. Some are much more complicated than the parathyroids. Like the pituitary. That's about the size of a cherry pit. It does so many things, we can't keep track of them all. But that's another whole story that will have to wait.

13

The Master Control

A few days ago I decided to find out about pituitary glands. That sounds a little strange at first. I didn't decide out of the clear blue sky to find out about pituitaries. My interest had been aroused by an operation a friend had had. The operation wasn't on the pituitary; it was on the parathyroid glands, which are part of the same system. But when I started finding out about the other glands, I kept stumbling on information about the pituitary. Apparently it's very important. That's why I decided to find out about it.

Most people probably don't know or care about their pituitaries. Ask people on the street how their pituitaries are and they wouldn't know what to say. Most people probably think that pituitaries are a very strange subject, hardly worthy of conversation. Most people don't know that the pituitaries are very important glands, hardly deserving to be ignored. Let me explain.

Your pituitary is a gland about the size of a cherry pit. It lies in your head beneath your brain and above the roof of your mouth. It's in that protected spot because it's so important. It controls all sorts of things that go on in your body.

Of course, this little gland doesn't move around your body, controlling it. Instead, it sends out chemical messages called hormones. These hormones travel in your bloodstream. They reach other glands, organs, and body cells and turn them on or off.

One important hormone the pituitary sends out is called the growth hormone, or GH. This helps you grow to a normal height. Too much GH would cause you to be a giant; not enough would make you a dwarf.

GH acts through your body cells. Through some complicated work it helps your cells form more tissue protein, and that makes you grow.

Your pituitary also sends out a hormone called TSH. This reaches your thyroid gland and makes it grow. Somehow, TSH also makes your thyroid produce a hormone. This hormone controls how fast your body burns the "fuel" it gets from the food you eat. That has an effect on how fat or thin, how active or inactive you are. If your pituitary didn't produce TSH, your thyroid wouldn't work right. Then you might burn up too much or not enough fuel.

But your thyroid also "talks back" to your pituitary. If you have a lot of thyroid hormone in your blood, your pituitary produces less TSH. With less TSH in your blood, your thyroid makes less hormone. So when there's less thyroid hormone in your blood again, your pituitary begins making more TSH. Then your thyroid. . . . On and on it goes. You probably have gotten the idea by this time that there is a delicate balance between your pituitary and your thyroid.

Your pituitary is in delicate balance with other glands as well. It produces a hormone called ACTH, which works on part of your adrenal glands. These glands then produce hormones that help keep the right amount of sugars and salts in your body. If you have too much or too little of certain salts in your blood you could become very sick. So, in a roundabout way, ACTH is responsible for keeping that in balance.

Your adrenal glands, by the way, produce more than thirty different kinds of hormones to keep everything in your body running smoothly. We don't know exactly how all of these work. We also don't know exactly how the pituitary controls some of the adrenal hormones and not others. We only know that it all works together well.

Your pituitary also controls the work of your kidneys by producing the hormone ADH. This hormone helps the kidneys keep water in your blood. If you lost the water, your blood would be too thick. You would have to drink hundreds of gallons of water every day just to stay alive.

By this time, you're probably convinced that your pituitary is a very important gland that controls many other glands, organs, and cells.

However, I haven't told you *half* of what your pituitary does. It's very complicated. It releases about a dozen different hormones. We don't understand all of them or just how they work; we only know, from the hormones we do understand, that all of them are probably very necessary to life.

But it becomes more complicated yet. Obviously, the pituitary can be called the master control gland because it influences so many other glands. But the pituitary doesn't act on its own. It is controlled by a part of your brain known as the hypothalmus. The pituitary lies close to the hypothalmus. There's some kind of two-way action between the hypothalmus and the pituitary. So the pituitary probably couldn't do its work and its control without its own master control, the hypothalmus.

You may have guessed that the story doesn't end even here. Something must control the hypothalmus. What makes that work? It's part of your brain, and your brain is very complicated. We probably will never understand it completely.

Someone much greater than we created our brains, which control our glands, which control our bodies. Perhaps you can call your pituitary the master control gland and your hypothalmus the master controller. But only God can be called the true Master Controller.

14

Help!

Have you ever been scared—really frightened? Maybe you almost had an accident on your bike. Or you may have been home alone and you heard something fall in another room.

When the whole thing was over—you swerved to avoid a car, or you found out what fell—you were probably shaking like a leaf. Your heart was pounding, your hands were cold, and you may have been pale.

You probably even made some comment like, "Here I am shaking like a leaf for nothing. How silly."

That's not silly at all. That's the way God created your body to react to emergencies. If you sense danger, even before you're really sure, your

Bishop 03

body will call, "Help!" Sometimes the danger signal may be a false alarm, but your body is ready, just in case. And it gets ready with lightning speed. Changes that you can't control happen instantly.

Your heart beats faster. If you're going to need muscle power, those muscles will need extra oxygen. Extra blood with that extra oxygen must reach your muscles. So your heart beats faster to pump blood around your body faster.

Within your muscles blood vessels expand. More blood with more oxygen pours through them. Also, all the arteries in your body tighten. This raises your blood pressure. Blood is almost slammed, with extra force, into your muscles.

In fact, your muscles change somewhat so that they won't tire as easily. In an emergency you can lift heavier objects or run faster or farther than you normally can. Your muscles are a little different. That's why you shake when the emergency is over. Your muscles are relaxing and trying to return to normal.

You often turn pale in an emergency. That's because the blood vessels in your skin shut down automatically. Blood which usually goes to your skin is rerouted to muscles and organs which need it. Healthy skin color doesn't help you in an emergency. Ready muscles do. That's also why you feel a little cold and clammy. Warm blood hasn't been flowing to your skin.

You're not aware of it, but your liver has gone automatically into high gear. It pours its stored sugar—instant energy—into your blood to be rushed to muscles and organs.

One set of organs slows down or stops in an emergency—your digestive tract. It really doesn't matter at that moment whether or not you digest your food. Your body will do that when the emergency is over.

Although your digestion stops, your lungs work overtime. Air passages within your lungs automatically widen. You take in more oxygen, which is rushed to your muscles.

And your eyes work a little harder. Your pupils—those black holes—become bigger to let in more light. So what if everything seems a little bright? It's important to see as much as possible.

Although you don't know it, your blood even changes a bit. It's able to clot more quickly. So, if you are hurt and do bleed, you won't lose as much blood as you might otherwise. Your blood will clot and stop the bleeding quickly. You may not have time at the moment to try to stop it yourself.

Isn't that amazing? All those changes are designed to help you meet an emergency. They happen in an instant, before you're even sure that there is an emergency.

All those changes are produced by two tiny glands called your adrenal glands. These glands rest on top of your kidneys (*ad* means "near," or "close to"; *renal* refers to your kidneys). Each gland is no bigger than your fingertip and weighs less than a nickel. Yet together they're powerful enough to make all those instant changes in your body.

Your adrenal glands make those changes by pouring a hormone, a chemical message, into your blood. That hormone is so powerful that about one-thousandth of an ounce—less than good-sized drop—can prepare you for an emergency.

How does your adrenal gland know when to put out that hormone? Well, it has a "hotline" to your brain. A series of nerves connects your brain and adrenal glands. When your brain shouts, "Emergency!" your adrenal glands respond. Most of your glands don't have "hotline." They're regulated by hormones. But your adrenal glands must produce instantly, so they're set up with faster communication lines.

Actually, when I say "adrenal," I really mean adrenal *medulla*, the inner part of that little gland. The adrenal *cortex*—the outer part of the gland—has entirely different work to do.

So, every time you sense an emergency, one little part in each of two little glands shouts, "Help!" Your body goes through instant automatic changes designed to help you protect yourself. You don't have to think about it or control it. All the right things simply happen.

That's not silly at all. That's wonderful. That's the way you were created. How can anyone deny that God designed your body?

15

Still More Trouble with George

"That George," she sputtered. "He doesn't have a brain in his head."

"Oh no, here we go again," I sighed to myself. "Continuing the same grand tradition."

Her "grand tradition" was to pick George apart piece by piece. I usually listened in silence, mentally picturing poor George minus some body part.

"He's spineless," she had said. I had seen George as a quivering lump of flesh.

"He doesn't have any nerve," she added later. The lump stopped quivering, in my mind.

But now, no brain? Poor George couldn't think about his sorry condition without a brain. He couldn't even live. In my mind she had just dealt

George his death blow. I couldn't let that pass. I decided to speak up.

"That's going a little far," I replied. "I'm sure he has a brain. It may not look like much. . . ."

A picture of George's brain flashed through my mind. I saw a grapefruit-sized, pinkish-grey, jelly-like mass. The top was all wrinkled, like a huge walnut, and the whole thing sat on a thick stem. True, it wasn't much to look at.

"Because it isn't much," she interrupted smugly. "Why, just yesterday. . ." But my mind was off again.

"Isn't much?" I wanted to shout. "Thirteen *billion* cells with *trillions* of connections isn't much?" If George's brain is at all normal for a human, he probably *does* have about thirteen billion cells in it. And each of those cells is connected to many, many other cells. Scientists can hardly comprehend those numbers. *How* parts of the brain work is a complete mystery to them. No one can say that George's brain isn't much.

The last time I saw George, we were at the grocery store. We carried on a perfectly normal conversation, although there was noise all around us. So I know that his reticular formation was in working order.

"Reticular formation" is a big name for a tiny part of George's brain. No larger than his little finger, this tiny group of cells keeps George sane, among other things.

All the messages that George receives from

seeing, hearing, smelling, tasting, and touching pass through that part of his brain. Unimportant information is stopped right there. Only important messages travel on to where he can really think about them. If George had to think about every single message his body received every single minute, he'd have far too much information to process. He'd go insane.

George was very sane the last time I saw him. In fact, his reticular formation told him that what I was saying was more important than the messages over the loudspeaker. Pretty good work for such a small part of the brain.

Of course, George was breathing and his heart was beating. He told me about a dinner he had just eaten, so I know that he was digesting food. And I suppose he was perfectly capable of coughing and swallowing. George's medulla was working.

That part of his brain is only as fat as his thumb, yet it helps keep George alive. Imagine what would happen if George had to tell his heart to beat and his stomach to work. He would never have talked with me if he had to concentrate on his breathing. George's medulla may not look like much, but it surely does a wonderful job all by itself.

George seemed very comfortable in that grocery store. He wore an overcoat, but it was cold outside and cool in the store. So George's hypothalmus seemed to be working.

No bigger than a kidney bean, that part of

George's brain called his hypothalmus is his body thermostat. It makes him shiver when he's cold and sweat when he's warm. It also can make George feel tired, thirsty, hungry, afraid, and jealous. No one knows exactly how that little part of his brain works. I do know that George feels all these emotions at times.

When I first spotted George at the store he was walking, pushing a cart, and grabbing a can from a shelf, all at the same time. Obviously, there's nothing wrong with George's cerebellum.

His cerebellum looks like a little ball of twine and lies at the back of his brain. It sends messages to all the muscles that George can control. George probably couldn't have done all those things when he was a baby. He had to *learn* to walk, *learn* to push a cart, and *learn* just how far to reach for that can. His cerebellum is a good learner. Because it's working so well, George doesn't have to think about those things as he does them.

Think! There's the key! I know that George is a good thinker. I've had some interesting conversations with him. I'm sure his cerebrum is fine.

The largest part of George's brain, his cerebrum, is responsible for the way George thinks, learns, remembers, and plans. It's the part that makes George George and not some animal. It's also one of the most mysterious parts of George's brain. Scientists spend lifetimes studying the cerebrum and still can't understand it. They draw maps of the cerebrum to tell which part controls speech, which part interprets sight, and so on. Yet they can't say exactly how it works. They only know that it is very complex, still very much of a mystery.

In fact, the whole human brain is a mystery. It's one of the true wonders of creations. All those parts—even more than I mentioned—working together in perfect harmony, leaves one almost speechless with awe.

Somehow it didn't leave me speechless this time. I *had* to speak up.

"You can't say it isn't much," I blurted. "George walks and talks and thinks. He feels hunger and pain and love and jealousy. His brain is absolutely amazing."

She stared at me in disbelief. Usually I don't talk back that much. "I know what you're saying," she stammered. "I only meant. . ."

This time *I* interrupted, "Besides that, I like George. He's a good guy. At least *his* heart is in the right place."

I hope that doesn't get her started again.

16

Sleep

Don't you just hate to go to bed sometimes? When people around you are doing interesting things, or when you've had such a nice day that you hate to see it end, it's hard to give up whatever you're doing and turn in for the night. To lie for several hours, totally unaware of what's going on around you, while other people are active and things are happening all over the world almost seems to be an inefficient way to live. Why can't we just keep on going? Why do we *have* to sleep?

Scientists think that we must sleep for our own sanity. Everyone has had a "crabby" day after a night without much sleep. That's just the beginning.

In an experiment, scientists tried to keep people

awake for more than four days. After they went through the "crabby" stage, these sleep-starved people began to forget things. Then they began to imagine they saw things that weren't there. Later some of them became violent, imagining that people were out to harm them. Most of these symptoms disappeared after a good night's sleep, but one man who had stayed awake for eight days didn't completely regain his sanity for two years.

Scientists have found that some animals simply die when deprived of sleep for too long. They agree that people too would die if forced to stay awake too long.

Maybe that's why God made our bodies the way he did. Maybe he knew that sometimes we wouldn't want to go to sleep, so he made our bodies to simply fall asleep against our will. We've all had the experience of really wanting to stay awake but not being able to. I like to think that's God taking care of our minds and bodies when we neglect them.

Sleep itself is interesting; it's a shame you can't be awake to enjoy it. When you sleep, you don't simply sink into a state of unconsciousness dotted with dreams for a while. You pass through definite stages.

First you begin to get drowsy and close your eyes. Your breathing and heartbeat become steady and your brain activity slows down. You're still aware of what's going on around you: if someone should ask you a question, you might answer or you might just grunt. You're really not sleeping yet. This is just pre-sleep.

As you enter stage one of sleep, you may feel an arm or leg jerk. This is common and usually doesn't wake you completely. Immediately you sink back into stage one. Your temperature, pulse rate, and blood pressure drop slightly, and you breathe still more slowly. You have some conscious thoughts but can't control them easily. It's a mixture of dreams and regulated thought. If someone spoke your name you'd probably wake up. If you don't wake up, you stay in stage one sleep for about ten minutes before sinking into stage two.

In stage two, your eyes begin to move slowly from side to side. Your body functions slow down even more, but your brain becomes more active. You begin to dream short, unconnected dreams. You remain in stage two sleep from twenty to thirty minutes before sinking into stage three.

In stage three your muscles totally relax and your pulse rate, temperature, and blood pressure fall even lower. Your brain activity slows a bit, although you may dream. If you do dream, you won't remember it when you wake up because you were so deeply asleep. Ordinary noises won't wake you, but the ringing of a phone might. After ten to twenty minutes in stage three, you sink into stage four.

In stage four sleep, your body slows down to the lowest levels it will reach. Your body temperature may have dropped a full degree. Your heartbeat is the slowest it will be, and your blood pressure is very low. If anyone were to wake you from a stage four sleep, you would ask, "Where am I?" It would take a very loud noise to waken you.

You probably stay in stage four sleep for about twenty minutes and then begin to drift upward, through stage three to stage two. Now, however, you are totally asleep. Your muscles are more relaxed than they were the first time you went through stage two. You begin to move your eyes back and forth again faster than you did before. Scientists sometimes call this stage REM (rapid eye movement) to distinguish it from the first time you passed through stage two. You may spend about twenty minutes in stage two again.

Thus far in about seventy minutes you have drifted from stage one sleep down to stage four and back up to stage two, or REM. Then you begin drifting down again for a second time. So the cycle continues—your body and mind taking care of themselves while you are totally unaware of it.

Each stage of sleep is important. If you're deprived of one stage of sleep, your body will automatically try to make it up.

Sleep is interesting and is absolutely necessary to our physical and mental health. Our minds aren't so powerful that they can work continuously without a rest. God has made us so that our bodies demand sleep to rest our minds.

I'm glad that the mind of God is so great that he never sleeps. I feel safe when I think that while I'm sleeping, he's watching over me.

17

A Tear Falls

A tear falls; one big, salty tear. It gathers in his eye and trickles down the side of his little nose. Soon a second tear follows the first, and a third, tracing a watery path down the little boy's cheeks. The tears tell everyone around the little boy that he is sad. Because they fall, he feels better, and he wipes the damp evidence from his cheeks.

When a tear falls, it washes the eye. There are glands in the outside upper corners of the eye socket, under a fold of eyelid. These glands form tears from water, salt, certain proteins, enzymes, and a little bit of oil. As a tear courses its way across the eyeball the water bathes the eye, the compounds of salt and protein help the eye to see better, the enzymes attack any bacteria on the

eyeball, and the oil helps to keep the tear from splashing down the cheek. Little tear ducts on the outside corners of the eyes collect tears that are not flowing too swiftly. Acting as drain pipes, these half-inch ducts channel the moisture into the nasal passages.

A tear forms every time the eye winks. When the eye closes to shut out dust or glare, a tear forms. When the eye blinks, a tear forms. Countless times every day, tears form, clean the eye, and evaporate or roll down the drain pipe. What an efficient eye-washing system!

When tears fall, the soul is also washed. Everyone has known the need to cry, either from physical pain or from an inner pain that only the soul can feel. Everyone has bit a quivering lip, trying to hold back the tears. And everyone has given in to tears and felt the relief they bring. Although tears may not ease the physical pain or right the emotional wrong, they can make you feel better inside for a little while.

Jesus cried. Sometimes real tears fell; he wept at the grave of his friend Lazarus. Other times, I think he wept only tears of the soul—like when the rich young ruler could not sell all that he had to follow him, or when Judas Iscariot left the Last Supper early to betray him.

During the last week of his life, how often he must have longed to cry. How many times, I wonder, did he cry only tears of the soul; when even Peter denied him, when the soldiers mocked him, and when his own divine Father left him all alone on the cross. How bitter those unshed tears must have been!

And I, able to feel only a tiny part of that grief he must have felt, realize that his tears of the soul were not only for Judas's betrayal, Peter's denial, and the soldiers' mockery, but also for mine. And I think of his sacrifice for me, and my weak response, often marred by my own betrayals, denials, and mockeries of him. And a tear falls.

18

Bathtub Prayers

I say my very personal morning prayers in the bathtub, so I call them my bathtub prayers. I don't mean to be disrespectful; it just seems natural. That's when I sit and review my schedule for the day. So it's natural for me to spread it all out before God. He knows better than I what's going to happen that day, but I still need to ask about what I have planned. "Please help me with this class. Give me patience with this group or the wisdom to make things clear to that group. That concert (or speech) tonight will fall apart without your help. Keep me calm through the day and help me to remember that you're always near."

I don't think I could start a day without my

bathtub prayers. I need to remind myself that God has promised to be with me. And I need that quiet time to ask for help and (in human terms) remind God of his promises. Then throughout the day I can add extra prayers. "This is the class I was worried about. I need an extra bit of wisdom." Or, "This is the time I need a little calming down."

My evening prayers are a little different. I try not to concern myself about the next day, but concentrate on the day just past. So those prayers are more thankful. God has seen me through another good day. I'm healthy and happy and everything went well. There were even some pleasant surprises along the day. "Thank you. It could have been different."

Of course, all days aren't perfect. Sometimes too many instruments break, or I lose my temper or make some big mistake. But then it's a measure of grace that God didn't let me know in the morning that this unpleasant surprise awaited me. Besides that, he saw me through whatever it was. "Thank you for not letting me see what was going to happen. I would have worried too much. And thank you for helping me through and bringing the end of this day."

My Monday morning bathtub prayers are longer than any other. It's the beginning of a week. Besides taking Monday step by step, I look over the whole week. "An activity planned every evening this week, and I don't know what else is going to happen. Help me not to wear myself down too much today. Help me to be ready for whatever happens."

But then, Saturday evening prayers are also long. "Thanks for the whole wonderful week. It was better than I expected." Sometimes, "Thanks for getting me through the week. And thanks for not letting me know that it would be that tough."

Sundays are a day apart for me. That's why my "week prayers" are on Saturday nights and Monday mornings.

I don't say special prayers often at the beginning or the end of months. Maybe a week is all I can handle in my day-to-day reviews. I can't think of a whole month when I'm praying about my everyday activities.

But the beginning of a year is different. I can't imagine starting a new year without a special prayer. That's usually a bathtub prayer for me. "What's going to happen this year? We're planning a trip next summer. Should we go? May I teach another year? Whatever weather comes this winter, keep us safe and help me to see some beauty in it. Please stay close. I need help in the big and the little things."

This always follows the end-of-the-year prayer from the night before. That's a lot like the end-of-the-day prayers, only broader. "Thank you for another wonderful year. So far, school has been better than I had hoped. Everything is going well this year. Thank for all the opportunities you gave us."

Of course, some years are not as good as others. Every other year lately one of my family members has died. But I can always say, "Thank you that I didn't know at this time last year that she was going to die." Or, "Thank you for being so very close during that death." And always, "Thank you for seeing me through another year."

One of those recent years was both good and not-so-good for me. My prayer on New Year's Eve reflected that. "Thank you for the wonderful father you gave me for so many years. And thank you that we didn't know ahead of time how hard his last months would be. Sometimes it's better not to know. Thank you for bringing dear friends close at just the right time, and thank you for. . ."

My beginning-of-the-year bathtub prayer was on Saturday morning. "Another year—I need you every step of the way. If all goes well, help me never to forget you. If there's trouble ahead and I can't see it, that's a mercy. Stay near." Of course it will be more personal than that. It will be, in my terms, a real bathtub prayer.

I suppose that many people have their bathtub prayers, personal calls for help mixed with special thank-yous. Maybe those prayers aren't always said in a bathtub, but they're still special, quiet moments between that person and God.

I can't think of starting a day without my bathtub prayer. How could anyone think of starting a year without it?

19

Squeezed into a Mold

I was born with two left feet. Not really, but so it seemed to me. Ever since I took my first baby steps, I've walked awkwardly. At first I always kicked my own ankles, by mistake of course. When I outgrew that, I stumbled a lot. Now I stay upright, but I still clomp when I walk.

I was also born with two left sides, or two right sides. I don't know which. I guess I'm sort of left-handed, but not really. I've never figured it out. I eat with my left hand and write with my right. Some things I do with either hand. It's never really bothered me. In fact, sometimes I've found it rather convenient. If I'm in a hurry, I can eat and write at the same time.

But I'm lousy at directions. Tell me to turn

left, and I have to stop and figure out which way that is. I usually give directions using "north" and "south." I'm good at that. But I could never figure out where left field was at a baseball game.

My arms are on crooked too. I couldn't throw a ball straight if my life depended on it. Nine out of ten bowling balls I've thrown have landed in the gutter. The last time I went bowling was about twenty years ago. After I threw one ball, I turned around to find everyone behind me choking back tears of laughter—or maybe they were tears of sympathy. Anyway, I never went again. I figured that there were other things I could do.

All of this awkwardness doesn't bother me at all now. In fact, I take a rather perverse pride in it. I figure it makes me unique, and I like to be unique.

I didn't like it when I was growing up, however. From about fifth grade on I felt the pressure to be like everyone else. Everyone else, I thought, threw balls straight, never mixed up their directions, and stayed firmly on their feet. So I really tried.

I never volunteered to pitch in a softball game. I knew better than that. I'd always head way out to left (or was it right?) field someplace and (honestly!) pray fervently that no balls would come in my direction.

I did try out for our junior high girls' basketball team once. I didn't really want to, but all my friends were trying out, so I did too. As part of the tryouts we had to run backwards the length of our school gym. Everybody else did it. I went partway and then lost my balance; I tried to do the rest from a sitting position on the floor. Deep down inside, I really was rather relieved, because then I knew I wouldn't make the team.

By that time I knew that I'd rather play my violin than play ball. I'd rather go to a concert than go to a game. I never said much about it because it seemed like the rest of the world (at least the kids my age) would rather play ball and go to a game.

Since then I've discovered that other kids in my class felt the same way. But they kept their mouths shut too because the pressure was on. We were all trying to be like everyone else. So we all went to games and tried to fit in.

I'll never forget my sister's high school graduation. It was a turning point for me. I was in ninth grade at the time.

Dr. Smedes spoke on Romans 12:2. He translated it into words I could understand: "Don't let the world squeeze you into its mold." Originally Paul had said that to the Roman Christians, warning them to avoid pagan practices. But that night he said it directly to me through Dr. Smedes.

My world certainly wasn't pagan, but it was squeezing me. And I was letting myself be squeezed. I didn't fit into this physical-perfection, high-interest-in-sports world. That wasn't me, so why pretend?

Besides that, Romans 2:1 talks about present-

BISHOP85

ing your body as a living sacrifice to God. Maybe for some people that meant lots of participation in sports. Maybe they figured they could perfect their bodies that way. But not me. Participation in sports for me meant mangling my body, forcing it to do things it wasn't made to do. Better for me simply to take good care of my body.

And Romans 2:4–8 talks about how different people have different talents. Everyone should develop his or her own talents. Physical coordination was not one of my talents. My talents and my interest lay in music and literature.

Those thoughts carried me through high school and beyond. I stopped going to games. I simply wasn't interested in them. I majored in music because I loved it.

Even now I'd rather watch a concert or a play on public television than see Monday night football on another channel. I'd rather talk about a book than about the latest baseball scores. I refuse to be squeezed into a mold.

Now I teach music in two Christian schools. Fine arts are very important to me. In fact, sometimes I find it hard to understand why they aren't important to more people. I'd love to see students discussing the latest concert just as they discuss yesterday's game. I'd even love to see an arts section in the daily newspaper instead of a sports section.

Well, maybe an arts section should appear *with* a sports section. Maybe we can discuss the concerts *and* the games. I shouldn't try to squeeze everyone into my mold, just as I shouldn't be squeezed into a mold.

After all, everybody is unique. We each have our own mold. No one should feel pressured to fit the wrong mold. And no one should try to squeeze anyone else into the wrong mold. Rather, as Paul said, we should develop our own talents and love each other as we are.

20

Oh Brother, Rose

"Wake up, everybody! There's a pink mountain outside!"

"Oh brother, who's that?" I wondered sleepily as I rolled over on my cot. "Whoever it is, she won't last long around here."

"Here" was our Peace Corps training camp. We had all traveled from different parts of the United States the day before. No one knew anyone else, and we were tired, hungry, and a little bit shy. Now we had to get up at 5:00 AM and look at a pink mountain? Oh, brother!

"My name's Rose," came the announcement from our self-appointed alarm clock. "Let's get acquainted."

I had Rose marked in my mind from that

morning on as someone a little bit "different." After all, who would wake up a roomful of strangers at 5:00 AM with an announcement about a pink mountain? Rose was lacking in the social graces, I thought.

I was sure that Rose was different after I had been around her for a few weeks. She never really bothered to comb her hair in any definite style, like the rest of the girls did. She didn't care about her clothes too much; she always wore khaki bermudas and a nondescript white blouse. Rumor had it that Rose had been in the Marines; she did have that plain, no-nonsense look about her.

Rose was a little older than most of the trainees, but she ignored that fact. She didn't seem to realize that people just a little bit older should maybe *act* just a little bit older.

On our daily hikes, Rose was right out there in front, not only plowing through the sugar cane, but asking questions about it along the way.

In language classes, Rose was always in there wrestling with the strange phrases, and even trying out new sentences.

In Asian studies, Rose wasn't content to listen to the lectures. She was always asking those questions that you think of but never bother to ask. Rose was just a little too "gung-ho." She always seemed to do her own thing at the time when doing your own thing wasn't the right thing to do. She was just a little "different."

For example, there was the incident in the

dining hall. A week after we arrived, we were instructed to speak only Malay during our meals. The first meal was awkward, to say the least. No one was about to make up a sentence in Malay yet. It just really wasn't the thing to do at that point. No one was speaking in the dining hall. Suddenly, in the silence a "Tolong saya garam" rang out (a mangled version of "Please pass the salt"). Oh brother, Rose was at it again!

Then there was the time we were supposed to start wearing sarongs—a long piece of cloth worn like a skirt and wrapped around the waist. I just couldn't get mine on right. It always bubbled in the back. Friends were trying to help me wrap it right, but we just weren't succeeding. Then Rose came by. "Here, let me see if I can help. Oh, I see the problem. You've got quite a shelf back there."

"Oh brother, Rose," I thought. "Don't you know it's not nice to comment on someone's figure that way?" But I did notice that she was the person who finally showed me how to wrap a sarong right.

I guess my opinion about Rose changed with the flashlight incident.

Frances and I were scheduled to get up at 4:30 AM one morning to take care of the livestock around the camp. Frances was also a little older than most of us, but she acted her age; so much, in fact, that she refused to get up that early. If the livestock were to be fed, I'd have to do it alone. Okay. I could do that, except that my flashlight batteries were dead. Rose stepped in and offered her flashlight.

The next morning, somewhere between the chickens and the cow, I put Rose's flashlight on the ground. Somewhere between the cow and the pig, I stepped on the flashlight—and broke it. Oh brother, now what?

Rose was really nice about it. "What's a flashlight?" she said. "That can be replaced." (She didn't bother to mention the fact that a replacement was many miles away and flashlights were a necessity around camp at night.) "I can do without it. It's people that count, and you were doing your best. Forget it. Just don't say anything about it."

So that's how Rose operated! She had been doing little things like that for trainees all along—just not saying anything about it. Meanwhile she was enjoying training exactly as she wanted to. What other people thought of her didn't bother her, but she thought of other people a lot, and did quiet little things to help. Boy, did I have her marked wrong! She may have been different from the rest of us, but she really was a lovely person. She wasn't worried about people liking her; she was just Rose, and she loved life and people.

I've lost track of Rose over the years, but I've never forgotten her. Whenever I meet someone who I think is a little "different" and I'm tempted to think "Oh brother," I stop short. Instead, I say to myself, "Wake up everybody, there's a pink mountain outside," and I think of Rose. And I'm glad that some people dare to be just a little "different."

21

A Gentile in the Promised Land

Third grade was a tough year for me. That was the year I realized that I was a Gentile. That was also the year I figured out that I did *not* live in the promised land.

Accepting the fact that I was a Gentile was the toughest. The day I realized it, I almost went home sick.

Our teachers had talked about God's chosen people. That was nothing new to me. I had always figured I was one of the chosen. We had also heard about Jews and Gentiles. In Jesus' time anyone who wasn't a Jew was a Gentile. Somehow a Gentile wasn't quite as good. I understood all that, but somehow I had never connected "God's chosen people" with the Jews.

I forget what that third-grade Bible lesson was about. I just remember hearing Miss Hofman refer to God's chosen people. Two sentences later she called the same people "Jews." I didn't hear another word she said. Everything swirled in misty circles around me as I put two and two together.

I knew I wasn't a Jew; I was Dutch. But there were only Jews and Gentiles. Oh my goodness, I was a Gentile! I was one of those not-quite-as-good people! I wasn't one of the chosen people the Old Testament talks about. I was dizzy the rest of the day. All I could think was, "I'm a Gentile, and I can't help it."

It didn't take me long after that to figure out that Grand Rapids was not the promised land.

I had long harbored hopes that maybe Jesus had walked on a little part of our backyard. I even went through a phase of not walking back there for fear I'd be treading on holy ground. However, I soon came to grips with the fact that I did not live in Israel. Jesus had never walked anywhere near Eastern Avenue.

Since I had accepted being a Gentile, living in Grand Rapids didn't really bother me. It would do, even if it weren't the promised land. Anyway, I could play in the backyard again because it wasn't holy.

As I grew up, I began to put things in order. I realized that the Old Testament Jews were God's chosen people, and I'd have to accept that fact. I also realized that God offered salvation to the

Jews first, but then to the Gentiles. And because I believed in Jesus, I was saved, even though I was a Gentile. In that sense I *was* one of God's chosen people.

As I grew up, I also began to dream of going to Israel and meeting real Israelites (or Israelis, as they're called now). If I couldn't live in the promised land, at least I could see it once. Besides that, I think I also wanted to see if there was anything special about the Jews. After all, God *did* choose them first.

When I finally went, I had a great time. I'd recommend it to anyone who likes to travel. I saw Jerusalem, Nazareth, the Mount of Olives, and many of the places the Bible mentions. It was inspiring, and it did help me understand some Bible stories just a little better. I also had some experiences I'll never forget.

I was mugged just outside of Nazareth. Cathy and I had lost our way. We were walking down some little out-of-the-way street when someone started following us. Suddenly he jumped on my back, pinned my arms down and started dragging me off the street. Cathy jumped on his back and screamed. I screamed, kicked, and bit. He let go and ran. We ran too, in the opposite direction.

That night we stayed at a convent. The nuns spoke only French; we spoke only English. Somehow we managed to communicate.

On our first day in Jerusalem we checked into a five-story hotel. It had no heat, no services, and no one in the dining room. We soon figured out

that we were the only guests in the whole hotel. Deciding that something wasn't quite right, we checked out two hours after we checked in.

After that we went to the YWCA in Jerusalem. All this time we had been traveling with two sets of clothes each. Every night we'd wash one set of clothes.

It was cold in Jerusalem, but the Y had heaters. So I washed my clothes and hung them in front of an open window, over the heater. That night the heat went off, and it snowed. I woke up to find my only clean set of clothes frozen solid.

I also became sick in Jerusalem and couldn't leave the Y for two days. I think it was some food I bought from a street vendor. I had eaten food from vendors in Calcutta, Singapore, Hong Kong, and even Katmandu. I figured I had an iron stomach, but the Jerusalem falafel did me in.

Anyway, all those stories are things that happen when you travel the way we did. I could have told stories to my friends back home about getting lost in Japan, sleeping in a mud hut in Nepal, or swatting bedbugs in New Delhi. But the stories I chose to tell were about the Israelis.

It was a long time before it dawned on me why I told those particular stories. I think I was trying to tell my fiends that Israelis are just like other people. I was really saying, "They're no better and no worse than other people. God didn't choose them first because he knew they'd be special. They're special only because he chose them first."

It took me longer yet to put my third-grade discovery and my travels in Israel all together. It had been hard for me to accept being a Gentile. I figured that made me second-best. So it was easy for me to tell stories about the Israelis. I figured that this showed them as no different from others.

But all along I was really telling stories on myself. After all, didn't Paul say that we're all Abraham's children spiritually? In other words, God didn't choose me because I'm so special. I'm special only because he chose me and I'm his. That makes me a very humble and a very thankful Gentile.

22

Rules

I always sat between Mom and Peg at the dinner table. Peg was eight years older than I, so I had a "big person" on either side of me to help pass the food. And I always sat at a certain corner because I ate left-handed.

Louise, who was only two years older, sat at the opposite corner of the table. She sat between Dad and Ralph so that they could help her.

Our positions at the table never varied. For years we all sat in exactly the same places.

And for years we always ate two meals together. Mom served breakfast at 7 AM and dinner at 6 PM, and we'd all better be there, or else. That was one of the rules.

Several other rules also applied to our family

meals. Among the most noteworthy were the Take-It-All, the Clean-It-Up, and the Try-It-Once Rules. Also enforced were the General-Interest Rule, the Last-Word Rule, and the One-Week-Right Rule.

The Take-It-All Rule dictated that we must sample everything on the table. Disliking a certain vegetable was no excuse. If it was served, we must eat it. After all, Mom and Dad explained, we should not become fussy eaters. Besides that, we might learn to like those foods we wanted to pass up.

I still remember the day Mom excused me from eating green beans. I was sixteen at the time. She said that maybe green beans were one food that I never would like. But up until then, whenever green beans had been served, I had been instructed to take some. I usually took one bean.

The Clean-It-Up Rule applied to our plates. Besides taking a bit of everything served, we were required to eat it. It was wasteful to leave food on our plates. We weren't allowed to waste food, so we must abide by the rule and clean up our plates. I always ate that one green bean I took. I learned how to stuff bits of it into my potato so that I wouldn't notice it.

The Try-It-Once Rule was a combination of the first two rules. If Mom served something new, we all had to take some and eat it. After the meal, we'd discuss the new food. Did we like it? Would we like to have it again? If the yeses outnumbered the nos it became a part of our diet. Then the Take-It-All and Clean-It-Up Rules applied to everyone, even to those who had voted no.

Hominy found its way onto our table only once under the Try-It-Once Rule. There were five no votes and one maybe, so Mom said that she'd never serve it again.

Exactly one week after we voted down hominy, our family went to visit Uncle Enno and Aunt Ruth in Chicago. As soon as we arrived, Aunt Ruth announced, "We have something very special for dinner tonight—hominy!" Without asking, we kids knew that the Take-It-All and Clean-It-Up Rules applied. We all took some hominy, and we all ate it. Afterwards, Dad and Mom said that they were really proud of us.

The General-Interest Rule was unique to our family, I think. It applied to conversation at the table. If one or two people started a conversation others found boring, someone else would say, "Subject is no longer of general interest." This meant, "Change the topic of conversation, please."

That rule worked every time. Anyone old enough to know what "Subject is no longer of general interest" meant was old enough to contribute to the conversation. But if you said "Subject. . . ," you had better have had an interesting topic to substitute or you'd have been stared down in stony silence. We always had lively conversations at the dinner table.

The Last-Word Rule applied only to the kids.

Dad always read aloud from the Bible when we were finished eating. To show that we had listened, we'd have to repeat the last word he had read.

Because I was the youngest, the Last-Word Rule was easy for me. The oldest would say it first, then on down the line. So, if the last word were *tabernacles*, I'd hear "tabernacles" (from Dad), "tabernacles (from Ralph), "tabernacles" (from Peg), and "tabernacles" (from Louise). If I couldn't have remembered the word after all *that*, something would have been dreadfully wrong.

Sometimes Dad would surprise us, especially if he thought we weren't listening. He'd stop halfway through, look straight at any one of us, and ask, "What did I just read?" If you didn't know, you'd really be in trouble.

The One-Week-Right Rule covered the saying of our prayers. Before and after each meal, after Dad finished praying, we kids would say our prayers aloud: "Lord, bless this food. . ." before, and "Lord, we thank thee for this food. . ." after.

As we grew up, one by one we decided that we were too old to say that prayer aloud. That's when the One-Week-Right Rule would go into effect. The person applying for silent prayer status was required to say his or her prayers correctly for one week before the request was granted. "Correctly" meant that it must be "bless *before* the meal and "thank" *after*. If we slipped up once, we started our week all over. We had to say both prayers correctly at fourteen meals to prove that we were old enough to say them silently.

The idea was that we had to prove that we were thinking about what we were praying. I think it took me about three weeks to prove that I thought while I prayed.

Of course we had more rules than those covering meals. We always let someone know where we were going when we left the house. We all carried our own house keys, and woe be to the person who lost a key. We were limited to ten minutes on the telephone and fifteen minutes in the bathroom. We cleaned our own bedrooms and helped with the other rooms. We took turns doing the dishes.

There was one exception to the dishes rule. Sometimes Louise and I would be scheduled to do them together. Mom would do them on those nights only if we spent that time playing duets on our violins—without bickering. As soon as we started to argue, the deal would be off and we'd find ourselves back in the kitchen doing dishes.

When I talk about all these rules now, you might get the impression that I was part of an overregulated family. I didn't feel that way at all. I knew that each rule was there for a good purpose, and I usually knew the purpose. Besides that, I knew that a family—like any group of people living together—needs rules. We all loved and respected each other, but family rules just made things run more smoothly. I was a part of the family, so I abided by its rules.

But the reason for all those rules went deeper than that. Mom and Dad both let us know that God had put us in that particular family. God has rules for our lives—think of the Ten Commandments—so we were to grow up knowing that there were rules to follow in life. Dad and Mom both felt it was their duty to bring us up the best that they could. They took Proverbs 22:6 seriously: "Train a child in the way he should go, and when he is old he will not turn from it."

Besides that, the rules worked. Now I can eat almost anything that's set before me. I've even smiled my way through soup with fish eyes in it. But I still eat my green beans hidden between bits of potato.

23

Goodbyes

I hate goodbyes. I'm not good at them. I never was. When I was young, the end of the school year was always difficult for me. I knew that I wouldn't see some of my friends all summer. I never said goodbye. Usually I said, "See you in September."

When I was fourteen, our family moved a few miles south of town. I avoided our neighbors for a week before we moved because I didn't think that I could say goodbye to them.

Saying goodbye to good friends who are moving far away is still more difficult. Who knows when you'll see each other again? It could be a year or more. I never manage those goodbyes well. Usually I cry, promise to write letters, and

say, "Keep in touch." I notice that I'm not the only person who cries in places like airports. Saying goodbye must be difficult for other people too.

When I left my friends halfway around the world, I knew that I'd probably never see them again. Yet I said, "Goodbye for now. I'll try to come back next year." That was an easy way out of a difficult situation. There were no tears, no final farewells, just "See you later." I simply couldn't say that final goodbye.

Absolutely final goodbyes are the most difficult to face. A friend or a loved one dies, and we must say goodbye. Everyone has trouble with that because it hurts so much. I've found that, in those cases, it's almost impossible to say goodbye.

I saw my brother the morning he had heart surgery. Of course I knew that he might die. But I smiled and said, "See you later." I did see him later, and I whispered goodbye, but it was too late. When my sister died, I thought I had learned my lesson. I knew that she was going to die, probably that night. So I kissed her and said, "I'll see you in heaven." That was better.

But those goodbyes don't become easier with practice. The last time I visited my father in the hospital, I kissed him and said, "See you tomorrow." Then I cried most of the way home, because I didn't know if he would have a tomorrow. He didn't.

I used to think that God showed us his grace in

giving us phrases such as "See you later." I thought that he knew how difficult goodbyes would be, so he gave us an easy way out.

It was also a bit of God's grace, I thought, that we don't know what the future holds. If a classmate were to move during the summer, but I didn't know, "See you in September" was easy. If I weren't to see friends for three years instead of one, but I didn't know, "See you next year" was as honest a goodbye as I could muster. It certainly was much easier than "See you in three years" or "Will we ever meet again?"

I was on the wrong track. It is only a little part of God's grace that he makes difficult situations easier, even the final, impossible goodbyes possible. That's just the beginning of his grace. We concentrate so much on the goodbyes that sometimes we forget a tremendously amazing fact: if we're Christians, we never have to say goodbye at all.

Every year we celebrate Good Friday and Easter. We will remember in very special ways that Jesus died for our sins and rose again. He paid for our sins so that we could live forever with him.

Although we celebrate Christ's death and resurrection in special ways on certain days, we remember them all year. That's why we're called Christians. We're saved by Christ's death and resurrection. That's the most important fact of our lives, now and forever. That's the most important fact of all Christians' lives.

My father, sister, and brother were Christians. Someday I'll see them again in heaven. I never really had to say a final goodbye. "See you in heaven" was more to the point. The absolutely final goodbyes were *not* absolutely final.

What about those long-term goodbyes, those that may stretch over years? There's the grace of being able to say, "See you later." The very special grace is knowing, if you are Christians, that you *will* see each other later, no matter what.

Even the short-term goodbyes are easier for Christians. You can always say, "I don't know when I'll see you again. Perhaps tomorrow. But even if that's not in God's plan, I *will* see you again."

Christians use this saying at times: "The Lord watch over you and me as we are absent one from another." That's appropriate. It doesn't say goodbye.

I don't like goodbyes. They're difficult to say, and they hurt because they sound final. So I've given up on goodbyes for a very good reason. Because of Good Friday and Easter, Christians never need to say goodbye.

24

Celebrate Life!

Be happy! Celebrate! Enjoy life! Christians can't be glum, have a negative outlook on life, or live as if the world is something to be avoided. God is in control!

Think of it—wherever you go in this whole wide world, God is there. If you really trust him, he's not there spying on you; he's there watching over you to make sure that no harm comes to his child. You could be walking in the dark a block from home, or canoeing down a river a hundred miles away, or trekking in a tropical forest half-way around the world. He's there just as surely as any flesh-and-blood friend, only he's much more powerful. God doesn't live only in your home town. His presence covers the world, so the whole world is yours to enjoy in the comforting presence of his protection.

Think of it—whatever you do in life, if you are really trying to live for him, he'll help you. Your horizons are not limited only by the common professions. He's given you special talents to develop for him—maybe writing, or singing, or building, or running, or governing. Whatever your natural inclinations and talents are, he's given them to you and will help you develop them. The world needs Christians in every walk of life. Your life and talents are yours to enjoy and develop, and he'll help you in doing so. Your scope and power are limitless with him.

Think of it—whatever you see and touch in this world is his. He made all the trees and fields and animals and hills. People shape the world for their own use, but the whole world is really God's. He made it for you to enjoy, to glory in, and to care for. Anything you use is God's. In his love for his people, he gave them an intricate, wonderful creation to enjoy.

Think of it—not only is this world built and owned by him, but the sun, billions and billions of stars around us, billions and billions of galaxies beyond us, and bigger stretches of space and universe than we can ever imagine are his. He created it all, and it was good. His presence fills it all, and he continually guides it all. Yet he is so great that while he guides more stars over more space than we can imagine, he also is personally interested in each of us, loving and caring for us.

Of all people, Christians should be the happiest. Our God loves us and gives us this whole, beautiful world to live in. He guides our lives and gives us more opportunities and talents than we realize. He promises to help us and protect us. Besides all that, he promises that this life is just a beginning. He promises us eternal life—a perfect life forever.

How can we not be happy? Enjoy! Live! Celebrate life!